MAYER SMITH

The Billionaire's Invisible World

Copyright © 2025 by Mayer Smith

All rights reserved. No part of this publication may be reproduced, stored or transmitted in any form or by any means, electronic, mechanical, photocopying, recording, scanning, or otherwise without written permission from the publisher. It is illegal to copy this book, post it to a website, or distribute it by any other means without permission.

This novel is entirely a work of fiction. The names, characters and incidents portrayed in it are the work of the author's imagination. Any resemblance to actual persons, living or dead, events or localities is entirely coincidental.

Mayer Smith asserts the moral right to be identified as the author of this work.

Mayer Smith has no responsibility for the persistence or accuracy of URLs for external or third-party Internet Websites referred to in this publication and does not guarantee that any content on such Websites is, or will remain, accurate or appropriate.

Designations used by companies to distinguish their products are often claimed as trademarks. All brand names and product names used in this book and on its cover are trade names, service marks, trademarks and registered trademarks of their respective owners. The publishers and the book are not associated with any product or vendor mentioned in this book. None of the companies referenced within the book have endorsed the book.

First edition

This book was professionally typeset on Reedsy. Find out more at reedsy.com

Contents

1	The Disguise	1
2	The Encounter	7
3	The Unexpected Bond	13
4	The Price of Truth	20
5	The First Test	27
6	The Shadow of the Past	34
7	The Conflict Within	41
8	The Moment of Betrayal	48
9	The Truth Hurts	55
10	The Wall Between Them	62
11	The Redemption Road	69
12	The Hidden Agenda	76
13	The Test of Faith	83
14	The Sacrifice	90
15	The Invisible World Revealed	97

One

The Disguise

Julian Westbrook stood at the threshold of his mansion, staring out at the sprawling estate that had been his life for as long as he could remember. The manicured lawns stretched endlessly, framed by towering oak trees that whispered in the wind. A life of excess, of wealth, of everything he ever wanted, and yet, none of it seemed real anymore.

He had it all. The private jets, the luxury cars, the world at his fingertips. His name was synonymous with power, influence, and success. But none of it had ever brought him the one thing he truly craved—genuine love. No, the women who circled him, the business associates who bowed to his every whim, none of them had ever seen him for who he was. They only saw the wealth, the status, the façade. And he had grown tired of it.

Tired of the masks. Tired of the charades.

The Billionaire's Invisible World

For the past few months, Julian had been wrestling with a decision that, even to him, seemed unimaginable. But now, standing in the grand hallway of his mansion, he knew it was time. Time to walk away. Time to disappear.

He hadn't told anyone—not his closest friends, not his loyal staff, and certainly not his parents. They would never understand. They would think him insane, ungrateful for the life he had been given. But the truth was, Julian was suffocating under the weight of his own success. Every time someone kissed his ring, every time a beautiful woman gazed at him with longing, he couldn't help but feel an emptiness that no amount of money could fill.

It had all started a year ago when Julian had met someone who had changed everything. Her name was Emily, a woman so ordinary, so real, that it was hard to believe she existed in his world. She wasn't interested in his wealth, his name, or his connections. Emily had simply seen him. Not the billionaire, but Julian, the man who yearned for something more.

Their first encounter had been nothing extraordinary—just a chance meeting at a local café in a part of town far from the luxury enclaves he usually frequented. But it had been enough. The way she had smiled at him, the way she hadn't recognized him, had felt like a breath of fresh air.

But the more he had tried to know her, the more he realized how impossible it was. How could he tell her that he wasn't just the man she thought he was? That beneath the tailored suits, the designer watches, and the carefully constructed persona, there was someone who had never known real love? That someone who didn't want to be loved for his money, but for who he truly was?

The idea had consumed him.

And so, after months of agonizing over it, Julian had made the decision. He would shed his fortune. He would disappear.

He glanced once more around the familiar space, his eyes lingering on the portraits of his ancestors that lined the walls. The legacy of the Westbrook family was steeped in opulence, and it had always been assumed that Julian would carry that legacy forward. But he had no desire to be the man everyone thought he should be.

With a deep breath, he turned away from the window and made his way up the grand staircase, his footsteps echoing in the silent mansion. He entered his private office, where his personal assistant had already prepared everything he would need for his plan.

In front of him, a large desk sat covered in papers, his financial records spread out across it. Julian's wealth was staggering, the result of years of calculated investments and strategic business moves. But today, none of that mattered.

He pulled open the top drawer and removed a small black book—a ledger of sorts. This was his secret plan. A list of everything he would need to leave behind. The luxury accounts, the properties, the cars, the business interests. Every single thing that had defined his life.

He smiled bitterly as he glanced through it. He had no intention of simply disappearing into the ether. No, he would create a new identity. One where his wealth, his status, his reputation, would be erased. He would become someone new.

The first step would be to sever his ties to his company, Westbrook Enterprises. His father, who had built the empire from the ground up, would never understand. But Julian knew it was necessary. He couldn't keep living in the shadow of his family's expectations.

He reached for his phone, dialing a number he had known all too well, but now, it felt foreign in his hand.

"Julian," came the voice on the other end, deep and authoritative, "what's the matter? You've been quiet for days."

It was Charles, his most trusted advisor, the man who had been with him through every major decision in his life. Julian hesitated for a moment, unsure how to begin.

"Charles, I'm resigning," he said, his voice steady despite the storm brewing inside him. "I'm stepping away from everything. I need to disappear."

There was a long silence. "Disappearing? Julian, what are you talking about? You've spent your whole life building this company. Your family—"

"I know," Julian interrupted, cutting him off. "But I can't do it anymore. I need to find something real. Something honest."

Another pause. "I don't understand. You have everything. Why would you throw it all away?"

Julian stared at the phone in his hand, his reflection staring back at him in the dark screen. "Because I've never had anything real," he said quietly. "Not since I was a kid. Not since… well, never."

There was a sigh on the other end. "I don't know what you're trying to do, but if you need help—"

"No," Julian said firmly, his decision made. "I'm doing this alone."

He hung up the phone and sat back in his chair, his heart pounding. He had crossed a line now. There was no going back.

His next step was simple—disappear completely. He had already made arrangements for everything. His private plane would take him to a small, anonymous town where no one knew his name. There, he would find a modest apartment, a new job, and build a life from scratch.

But even as the plan took shape in his mind, a part of him felt a cold dread creeping in. What if it didn't work? What if he couldn't live without his old life, without the comforts he had taken for granted? What if, in trying to escape the chains of his wealth, he only ended up more isolated and alone?

But those thoughts were fleeting. He had made his choice.

As he left his office and made his way to the garage, he couldn't shake the feeling that this was more than just a simple escape. It was a quest for something deeper, something he could never find in the glittering world he had inhabited.

Julian Westbrook, the billionaire, was no more. The man who had been born into luxury and success was about to walk away from everything he had ever known, and into a world of uncertainty, where he hoped—just hoped—that he might finally find the one thing that had always eluded him: real love.

The engine of his car roared to life as he drove away from his mansion for the last time. Behind him, the gates of the estate closed, shutting out the world he had known for so long. Ahead, the unknown stretched out like an endless road, dark and winding, with no guarantee of what awaited at the end.

But for the first time in his life, Julian felt alive.

And that was enough.

Two

The Encounter

Julian had been in this city for exactly three days, and already, he was beginning to question his decision. The anonymity he had craved so desperately felt suffocating, like a cage that had been built by his own hands. The small apartment he had rented, tucked away in a nondescript building, was stark and uninviting. He had never lived in a place like this—cold, utilitarian, with none of the warmth he had grown accustomed to in his mansion. But this was the price he had to pay for freedom, or so he told himself.

The apartment's décor consisted of only the bare essentials: a small kitchen table, a couch that was more functional than comfortable, and a bed that felt too small for someone used to sprawling, luxurious spaces. It felt wrong in every way, and yet, Julian knew he had to keep going. The harder it was, the more it meant he was doing the right thing.

He'd spent the past few days sorting out the logistics of his new life—finding a job, learning to live without the conveniences of wealth, adjusting to the smallness of his new existence. The hardest part had been forcing himself to leave behind his credit cards, his business deals, the constant stream of money that had always been within his reach. Without it, he felt like a ghost, walking around a city that was too big, too loud, and too real.

But it wasn't the lack of wealth that unsettled him the most. It was the loneliness. The isolation that came from being no one. When he had been Julian Westbrook, people had sought him out. Women had approached him, businesses had courted him, friends had clamored for his attention. But now, as the man he had created—a man with no name, no ties—he was invisible.

And it was on this third day of his self-imposed exile that he finally ventured out into the world for a simple reason: he needed food. The refrigerator in his apartment was empty, save for a few beers and a carton of eggs. He hadn't yet learned how to shop for himself without the help of his house staff, and it was time to remedy that.

The streets were crowded with people rushing from one place to the next. Julian felt like an outsider, watching the ebb and flow of lives that weren't his own. He blended into the crowd, careful not to draw attention to himself, careful not to make eye contact with anyone. It was a strange feeling—the anonymity. At one moment, he would think he was invisible, and then, in the next, he would feel the weight of every gaze that passed him by.

The Encounter

He wandered through the bustling city center, unsure of where to go, until he spotted a small café on the corner of a busy intersection. The sign hanging above the door read "Emily's Café," written in simple, handwritten letters. There was something inviting about the place, something genuine, and Julian found himself walking in without thinking twice.

Inside, the café was warm and smelled of fresh-brewed coffee and baked pastries. The walls were adorned with local art, the tables scattered with mismatched chairs, giving the place an eclectic, cozy atmosphere. There were a few people sitting at the tables, but it wasn't crowded. Julian was used to places that were always full, always teeming with people vying for his attention, but here, in this little café, the world seemed to slow down.

He approached the counter, where a young woman with dark hair tied into a messy bun was arranging a stack of coffee cups. Her focus was on the task in front of her, and she didn't look up when Julian approached.

He cleared his throat. "Excuse me," he said, his voice low and uncertain, a far cry from the confident tone he had always used. "I'll have a coffee, please."

She glanced up then, meeting his eyes for the briefest of moments, before returning her gaze to the counter. "What kind of coffee?"

"Just black," Julian said, instinctively reaching for his wallet, but then he stopped himself. No, he didn't want to rely on anything that could give him away. He was just another man now, another face in the crowd.

"Coming right up," she said, not even giving him a second glance as she began to pour the coffee. Julian watched her for a moment, intrigued. There was something about her—her presence was so unaffected, so grounded. She moved with purpose but without haste, as though the world outside the café didn't matter.

It was rare to see someone so content in their own skin, someone so disconnected from the frantic energy of a city like this. Julian's thoughts were interrupted when she slid the cup toward him, her eyes still not meeting his.

"That'll be two fifty," she said, her voice soft, but with an edge of firmness that suggested she wasn't about to be manipulated by anyone, not even a man who looked like he could afford the whole café if he wanted to.

Julian handed her the money, and for a moment, their fingers brushed. There it was again—her presence. The energy between them felt electric, as though something had just sparked in the air. She didn't seem to notice, though, her eyes still focused on the change she was counting.

He stood there for a moment longer, unsure of what to do next. Should he leave, like a normal person? Or should he say something, ask her something that could break the silence, the barrier between them? For the first time since arriving in this city, Julian felt… unsure.

"Do you come here often?" he asked, the words spilling out before he could stop them. It was a stupid question, a question that people like him didn't ask. But something about her had made him throw caution to the wind.

She looked up at him now, her expression unreadable. For a moment, there was a flicker of something—curiosity, perhaps—but then it was gone. She shrugged. "Yeah, I work here. Not much else to do."

"I see," Julian said, his voice trailing off. It was the most ordinary of conversations, but there was something about the simplicity of it that felt like a lifeline.

"What's your name?" he asked, before he could stop himself.

She hesitated, a slight shift in her posture, before answering, "Emily."

"Emily," he repeated, the name tasting unfamiliar on his lips. It was such a simple, common name, yet to him, it sounded like a melody. "I'm Julian."

She nodded and turned away to tend to the other customers who had begun to trickle in. Julian stood there for a moment, unsure of what to do. He hadn't expected the conversation to end so abruptly, but he didn't mind. For some reason, he was content to watch her move around the café, a sense of calm settling over him.

He took his coffee to a small table by the window and sat down.

His mind raced, but for the first time in a long while, it wasn't because of business or money. It was because of her—because of Emily. There was something about her that felt real, something that he hadn't encountered in a very long time.

The more he watched her, the more he wanted to know her. But how could he? He wasn't Julian Westbrook anymore. He was just a man, a nameless face in the crowd. And for the first time, he realized that maybe that was enough. Maybe it was enough to be just a man who could fall for someone without the weight of his past pulling him down.

But as he sat there, watching Emily move through the café, a thought gnawed at him, a warning that something wasn't right. He had no idea what it was, but something told him this was just the beginning.

Three

The Unexpected Bond

The following days bled into one another, each one indistinguishable from the last. Julian found himself at Emily's café every morning, despite himself. It wasn't just the coffee, though he had come to appreciate the rich, comforting warmth of it. It was the way the mornings felt different when he sat there, a quiet observer of a world he had once known but now found himself disconnected from.

At first, his visits were brief, barely long enough for a cup of coffee and a polite exchange. But then something began to shift. Emily's presence was magnetic, though she hardly seemed to notice him. She was efficient, yes, but also gentle in a way that didn't fit the rough edges of the world around her. Her smile, when she did offer it, was small but genuine, and her eyes—there was something about her eyes, a depth that suggested she had seen things most people couldn't even imagine.

One morning, as he entered the café, the familiar hum of conversation and the clink of coffee cups felt more comforting than ever. Julian took his usual seat by the window, not expecting anything beyond his quiet observation. But today, Emily walked over, her brow furrowed slightly as she glanced at him.

"You're early today," she remarked, wiping her hands on her apron as she approached. There was an amused glint in her eye, but also something more—curiosity, perhaps.

Julian looked up from his coffee, caught off guard. He'd never intended to develop any sort of connection with her, but here he was, looking into eyes that seemed to see straight through him. "I guess I couldn't sleep," he said casually, shrugging as if it was nothing. "Thought I'd get some fresh air."

"Not much of a morning person?" she asked, the smile on her lips softening.

He shook his head. "Not really. I usually leave all the mornings to other people." The words slipped out before he could stop them, and for a moment, he regretted being so honest. It was a rare thing for him to open up about anything.

Emily didn't seem to mind, though. She sat across from him, as if this was an ordinary conversation between old friends. It was a strange feeling—this sense of ease with someone he had only just met. But Julian was too tired to try and dissect it. His life had been nothing but masks and pretenses, and in these moments with Emily, he could finally breathe.

"I get that," she said after a pause, her voice quieter now. "I wasn't much of a morning person either, but…" She trailed off, her gaze drifting to the door as if something beyond it had caught her attention.

But Julian was intent on her words. "But?" he pressed, leaning forward slightly. "But you got used to it?"

She smiled again, but this time, there was a faint sadness to it, a hint of something she hadn't yet shared. "Yeah, something like that," she said softly. "Life doesn't give you many choices, does it? Sometimes, you just have to do things because they need to be done."

Julian felt his chest tighten at the implication in her words. She wasn't just talking about mornings; she was talking about something far deeper, something he could only begin to grasp. It was a look, a tone, that sent a shiver down his spine. Emily had layers—more than she was willing to show on the surface.

He opened his mouth to say something, but before he could, the bell above the door jingled as a man entered, pulling Emily's attention away. She stood up, offering a quick smile to Julian as she turned to greet the newcomer.

Julian watched her with a mix of admiration and unease. He wasn't used to feeling like this. Normally, he was the one who controlled the room, who commanded attention. But with Emily, it was as if the air around her shifted in subtle ways that made him feel small, vulnerable even. And for reasons he didn't entirely understand, he didn't mind it.

As the man settled into the seat at the counter, Julian turned his attention back to the window, watching the people passing by on the street. He felt oddly restless, as if the world around him had sped up while he remained frozen in place. He had chosen this life—this quiet, anonymous existence—but now, with every day that passed, it seemed more and more like a cage.

The next morning, Julian arrived earlier than usual, hoping to catch Emily before the café became too busy. He wasn't sure what he was hoping for, but he felt an undeniable pull to understand more about her. More than the smiles and the small talk, more than the fleeting moments where their worlds briefly intersected. He wanted to know who she was beneath the surface.

When he walked through the door, he found her sitting behind the counter, her head buried in a book. It was a rare sight, considering how often she was moving around, serving customers and keeping the café running smoothly. She looked up at the sound of the bell, her eyes widening slightly when she saw him.

"Oh, you're early today," she said, marking her place in the book with a finger before placing it down. "Everything okay?"

"Yeah, just…" He hesitated. "I thought I'd get some peace and quiet before the rush."

She studied him for a moment, as if weighing his words. Then, without a word, she slid a cup of coffee across the counter toward him, her gaze never leaving his face.

"On the house," she said simply. Her voice was soft, but there was a warmth to it that made Julian feel like she was offering him more than just a drink. It was as if she was giving him permission to sit with her, to be present in a way that felt unfamiliar and unsettling.

He took the cup from her, feeling the heat seep into his palms. "Thanks," he muttered, unsure of what else to say.

Emily didn't return to her book immediately. Instead, she leaned on the counter, her arms crossed loosely as she observed him with an intensity that made Julian squirm in his seat. "You've been coming here every day for the past week," she said quietly. "What's your story, Julian?"

The question took him off guard. He had been careful, deliberately vague in all their previous conversations, but now it seemed like Emily could see right through him. There was no avoiding it. She wanted more than the polite, surface-level exchanges they had been having.

Julian set the cup down on the counter, his fingers brushing against the rim as he searched for the right words. "I'm just a guy," he said after a long pause. "Trying to figure things out."

"Everyone's always trying to figure things out," Emily replied, her tone dry. "But why come here? There are plenty of other cafés in the city. What is it about this one that keeps bringing you back?"

He could feel her gaze probing, but instead of feeling cornered, he felt... understood. It was an odd sensation, like she had touched a part of him he didn't know existed. He should've lied. He should've given her some fabricated story to explain his presence, but the truth was, he didn't know. Maybe it was her—her quiet strength, the way she moved through the world as if she didn't need anything from anyone. Or maybe it was simply that for the first time in weeks, he didn't feel alone.

"I guess it's the way you make things seem simple," he said finally. "Like it's okay to just exist without all the... other stuff. The expectations, the pressure."

Emily's eyes softened slightly, and for a fleeting moment, Julian thought he saw a flash of something vulnerable behind her usual composure. "I get that," she said quietly. "I've been where you are."

Her words were unexpected. Julian's mind raced, trying to figure out what she meant. Was she talking about some hardship in her past? A loss, perhaps? Something that had shaped her into the person she was today?

Before he could ask, the bell above the door jingled again, signaling the arrival of another customer. Emily straightened up, her professional demeanor returning as she moved to serve the new arrival. But something had shifted. Julian could feel it, the connection between them deepening in a way he hadn't anticipated.

As the day wore on, Julian stayed longer than he had planned, sipping his coffee, lost in thought. The café had become a place of refuge for him, a space where he didn't have to wear the mask he had grown so accustomed to. For the first time in a long time, he felt like he could just be.

And he wasn't sure what that meant, but he knew one thing: whatever had begun between him and Emily, it was something unexpected, something he couldn't walk away from.

And that scared him more than anything else.

Four

The Price of Truth

The days blended together, each one becoming more tangled than the last. Julian Westbrook's new life, the one he had so desperately sought, was not turning out as he had imagined. There was a silence to it, a stillness that gnawed at him. It was not the freedom he had expected. No, this was something far more unsettling—an emptiness that expanded with every passing hour.

Every morning, he returned to Emily's café, the ritual now ingrained in his routine. She had become the constant in his otherwise disorienting world. She was always there, with her easy smile, her quiet presence. She didn't push him to reveal more about himself, yet she saw right through the walls he had built. The way she looked at him—sometimes with understanding, other times with quiet skepticism—made him feel both seen and invisible at once.

That was the way Emily made him feel. She never asked too many questions. She simply allowed him to exist in her space, at her pace. But it wasn't long before Julian realized that the walls between them, though invisible, were there nonetheless. They had to be.

He had lied from the very beginning. The man she saw, the man who came to her café every day, was not Julian Westbrook, the billionaire. He was just a man—someone without a past, without any wealth or status. But for all his attempts to escape his identity, Julian knew deep down that the truth always had a way of resurfacing. It wasn't a matter of if it would come out, but when. And when that day came, when Emily discovered who he truly was, what would be left of the connection they had forged? Would she feel betrayed, deceived? Or would she understand?

The questions weighed heavily on him, and he couldn't stop asking them. Every interaction with Emily, every conversation, every smile she sent his way, only added to the growing tension inside him. He wanted her—he wanted to be the man who could open his heart to her, to give her everything he had, but there was a fundamental lie between them. That lie sat at the core of their relationship, thickening with each passing day.

It was just after noon when Julian walked into the café that afternoon, his usual cup of coffee in hand. Emily was behind the counter, but her usual cheery demeanor was absent. She looked preoccupied, her eyes distant as she wiped down the counter, her movements mechanical.

"Hey," Julian said, stepping closer. "Everything okay?"

She looked up, startled for a moment before forcing a smile. "Yeah, just busy. Same old."

He could tell she was lying. The tension in her voice, the way her shoulders were tight with something unsaid, was unmistakable. Julian placed his cup on the counter and leaned against it, studying her intently. There was something different about her today, something that unsettled him.

"You sure?" he asked, his voice softer this time.

Emily paused, looking at him with a mixture of hesitation and frustration. She placed the rag she had been holding down on the counter and took a step back, crossing her arms as she finally met his gaze. Her eyes were no longer the welcoming, soft eyes he had come to rely on. There was something else in them now—something raw, something that spoke of confusion, of hurt.

"I know you're not who you say you are," she said quietly, almost too quietly, as if afraid someone might overhear. The words hung in the air between them, and for a split second, Julian felt as if the ground beneath him had shifted. The world around them blurred, and all he could focus on was the piercing clarity in Emily's voice.

He swallowed, suddenly aware of how cold the room had become. His palms were clammy, his heart beating faster. "What do you mean?" he asked, though he already knew the answer. He had been waiting for this moment, even if he hadn't been prepared for it.

She took a deep breath, her eyes narrowing with an intensity he hadn't seen before. "I'm not stupid, Julian. I've noticed the way you don't talk about your past. I've noticed how you never mention where you live, what you do. You just show up here every day like it's some kind of escape. But I've seen the way people look at you. You think I haven't noticed?"

The accusation hit him harder than he expected. He had been careful—so careful—but somewhere along the way, he had let his guard down. He had gotten too comfortable in this strange, new life. Too comfortable with Emily. And now, in the face of her suspicion, his carefully constructed world felt like it was crumbling.

"I don't know what you're talking about," he said, though the words felt hollow in his mouth. He wanted to deny it, to keep up the pretense. But his voice betrayed him, faltering as his eyes met hers. She was waiting, watching him with those sharp, unflinching eyes.

"I'm not asking for your life story, Julian," she said, her voice low, but insistent. "But I know there's more to you than the guy who comes in here for coffee every morning. I don't know who you're running from, but I'm not going to sit here and pretend I don't see it."

The truth hung in the air like a suffocating fog. Julian opened his mouth, but no words came out. What could he say? That he was a billionaire who had given it all up to find something real? That he had built an entire life on a lie and had walked away from everything in search of love? How could he possibly explain all of that in a way that wouldn't make her hate him?

"I'm not trying to hurt you," he finally said, his voice breaking slightly. "I'm just... I'm trying to figure out who I am. What I want. And I didn't want to bring all of that—" he gestured vaguely, "—into this."

Emily's expression softened for a moment, the hardness in her eyes melting away just enough to show the hurt that lay beneath it. She glanced away, looking out the window as she sighed deeply. "I don't know if you're trying to protect me or yourself, Julian," she said, her voice trembling ever so slightly. "But you can't keep pretending like this forever. You can't keep hiding from the truth."

Julian took a step back, the weight of her words settling into him like lead. "You're right," he said quietly. "You're right. I can't. But it's not just my truth to tell."

She looked up at him then, her face unreadable. "What does that mean?"

He hesitated, feeling the familiar ache in his chest—the one he had been trying to outrun for so long. He had wanted to tell her, wanted to be honest, but the consequences had always loomed large in his mind. And now, faced with the inevitable, he couldn't help but wonder if it was too late.

"I'm Julian Westbrook," he said, his voice barely above a whisper. "I'm the heir to Westbrook Enterprises. I was born into money—into power. And I ran away from it all. Because I didn't want to be that person anymore."

The words tumbled out in a rush, as if they had been waiting to be released for far too long. Emily didn't say anything at first. She didn't move, didn't even blink. For a long moment, she just stared at him, her face unreadable. The silence between them stretched on, thick and heavy.

"You're a billionaire," she said finally, her voice soft, almost in disbelief. "And you've been lying to me this whole time."

Julian's heart sank. "I didn't mean to lie to you. I just—" He stopped, unable to find the words. How could he explain it to her? How could he make her understand why he had done what he did?

"Why, Julian?" Emily asked, her voice cracking slightly. "Why did you hide from me? From everyone?"

"I thought… I thought I could find something real," he whispered. "Something not based on money or power. Something just… honest."

Emily's eyes softened, but the hurt was still there, hidden beneath the surface. "And now?"

Julian swallowed, the weight of his own truth pressing down on him. "Now, I don't know if I've ruined everything."

The silence that followed was deafening. Emily didn't speak, didn't move. She just stood there, her arms crossed tightly over her chest, as if trying to protect herself from the storm that was brewing between them.

And in that moment, Julian realized something he had known all along: the price of truth was far higher than he had ever anticipated.

He had come to find love, but in the process, he had uncovered something far more painful—the cost of honesty. And now, he had no idea if he could afford it.

Five

The First Test

The days following Julian's confession to Emily felt like a fog had descended over his world, clouding every thought, every decision. He had expected the truth to be liberating, to free him from the weight of the lies he had carried for so long. Instead, it had felt like he was drowning in it.

Emily hadn't spoken to him much after that moment in the café. She had gone back to her usual routine—serving coffee, chatting with customers, moving through the motions as though nothing had changed. But Julian knew better. He could feel the distance between them, the invisible barrier that had been erected in the wake of his confession. It was as if the very air around them had thickened with the weight of unspoken words.

Every day, Julian returned to the café, hoping for some sign that things might go back to the way they were. He didn't expect things to be the same—not exactly—but he had hoped that Emily might at least acknowledge the bond they had begun to form, however fragile it was. Yet, every day, it felt more and more like he was just another customer to her, another nameless face in a sea of regulars.

On the fourth day after the truth had come out, Julian walked into the café, his heart heavy with anticipation. The bell above the door jingled as he entered, and he scanned the room for Emily. He found her behind the counter, her back turned as she prepared a cup of coffee for a customer. He hesitated for a moment, then made his way toward the counter, trying to suppress the knot that had formed in his stomach.

When Emily turned around and saw him, she offered a small, polite smile. It was the same smile she had given him a hundred times before, but there was no warmth in it now. No spark of recognition, no trace of the connection they had shared just days before. Julian felt a pang of disappointment, but he swallowed it down and forced a smile of his own.

"Morning," he said, his voice too loud in the quiet café.

"Morning," she replied, her tone flat. She gestured toward the menu above her head. "What can I get you today?"

Julian hesitated. "The usual."

"Coming right up," she said, turning back to the coffee machine without another word.

The First Test

Julian stood there for a moment, watching her, his heart sinking. This was it, he realized. This was the first test, the first real challenge in the aftermath of his truth. And it was going just as he had feared.

He had known, deep down, that Emily would need time. But there was something about the way she had distanced herself from him that stung, something that made him feel as though all the progress they had made had been for nothing. He had been so certain that their connection meant something, but now, standing in front of her, he wondered if he had been fooling himself.

As Emily handed him his coffee, their fingers brushed, and for a fleeting moment, Julian thought he saw something in her eyes—something soft, something vulnerable. But it was gone as quickly as it had appeared, replaced by the familiar, guarded expression she had been wearing since that day.

"Thanks," Julian said quietly, his hand shaking slightly as he took the cup.

Emily nodded and turned away, already focusing on the next customer. Julian wanted to say something, anything, to break the silence, but the words wouldn't come. He could feel the weight of his own guilt pressing down on him, suffocating him. What had he expected? That Emily would forgive him instantly? That everything would go back to normal just because he had been honest?

He glanced around the café, looking for a distraction. He wasn't ready to leave, not yet. But he knew that staying here would only make the tension more palpable. As he stood there, caught between wanting to stay and wanting to escape, the door jingled again, signaling the arrival of a new customer.

A man walked in, tall and broad-shouldered, with a confident air about him. He wore an expensive jacket, the kind Julian had worn a thousand times before—tailored to perfection, the fabric rich and immaculate. The man scanned the room, his eyes landing on Emily, who was still behind the counter.

Julian watched as the man approached her, his gaze fixed on her in a way that made Julian's stomach twist. There was something about the way the man looked at her—something predatory, something that made Julian want to step forward and claim her attention before the man could.

Emily, however, didn't seem to notice. She greeted the man with her usual professional demeanor, offering him a smile as she asked what he would like.

But Julian could see it—he could see the way the man was leaning in just a little too close, the way his hand lingered on the counter as he spoke to her. Emily, to her credit, remained polite and professional, but Julian could see the flicker of discomfort in her eyes, the way she shifted slightly, pulling back just a fraction as the man's presence seemed to encroach on her personal space.

Julian's blood began to boil. He didn't know what it was about this man—perhaps it was the way he was too confident, too familiar with Emily, or perhaps it was the fact that this man had something Julian didn't: the kind of life Julian had left behind. The wealth, the power. The things Emily might be drawn to, the things that had always been his, but were now nothing more than a distant memory.

Before he knew it, he was walking toward the counter, his hands gripping the edges of his coffee cup so tightly that his knuckles ached. The man was still talking to Emily, but Julian's gaze was fixed on him now, and he could feel the tension in the air, thickening with every step he took.

He stopped just behind the man, close enough to hear their conversation but far enough away to remain unnoticed. The man was laughing now, leaning in even closer, and Julian felt his teeth grit with frustration.

"I've got a place just around the corner," the man was saying. "I could show you sometime. We could grab a drink. You look like you could use a break."

Emily shifted again, her discomfort palpable now. "Thanks, but I'm fine," she said, her voice polite but firm.

The man didn't take the hint. "I insist. You know, you're different from most of the people I meet here. You're real. I like that."

Julian felt a surge of possessiveness that he hadn't expected. The man was getting too close, crossing boundaries Julian didn't even know he cared about until now. He knew he was being irrational, that he had no right to intervene. But in that moment, something inside him snapped.

"Is everything alright here?" Julian's voice was cold, sharper than he intended.

The man turned around, his expression momentarily surprised. "Oh, didn't see you there," he said, his tone condescending. "Just making some small talk with the lovely barista."

Emily gave Julian a quick glance, her expression unreadable, but Julian could see the tension in her shoulders, the way she stood just a little straighter. She was grateful for his intervention, but also uncomfortable with the attention it was drawing.

"I think she's fine," Julian said, his voice firm now, almost a challenge. He wasn't sure why, but he couldn't help himself. The man's smirk told him everything he needed to know—this wasn't a conversation that was going to end well.

The man took a step back, raising his hands in mock surrender. "No harm done, my friend. I'll see myself out."

As the man turned and walked toward the door, Julian felt a strange mixture of relief and frustration. Emily was still standing behind the counter, her eyes lowered as she cleaned a cup. Her silence spoke volumes, and Julian knew he had just made things worse.

He had acted out of impulse, out of jealousy, and it had only pushed Emily further away. She had never asked for his help, had never shown any sign that she wanted him to protect her. And yet, he had stepped in anyway, unable to stop himself.

Emily finally looked up, meeting his gaze with a mixture of gratitude and confusion. "Thank you," she said quietly, her voice soft, almost hesitant.

Julian nodded, his throat tight. "I didn't mean to… to make things awkward."

She shrugged, offering a small, forced smile. "It's fine. I've had worse."

For a long moment, neither of them spoke. Julian could feel the unspoken tension between them, thicker now than it had been before. He had passed the first test, but the price had been steep. He had acted on impulse, trying to protect her, and it had cost him. Emily was no longer the woman who had shared coffee and quiet moments with him. She was someone else now—a woman with her own life, her own boundaries—and Julian wasn't sure if he had crossed them.

As he turned to leave the café, the weight of his actions settled over him. The truth was out now, but the path to redemption, to regaining her trust, would be far harder than he had ever anticipated.

The first test had come, and he had failed.

Six

The Shadow of the Past

Julian couldn't shake the feeling that something was closing in on him, creeping closer with every passing day. It had started the moment he had intervened with that man in the café—the way Emily's eyes had met his, a mixture of gratitude and wariness, as if she were questioning whether she could still trust him. It wasn't the first time he had made a mistake, but it was the first time it had mattered this much.

The truth was, he was afraid. Afraid that his past would catch up with him in ways he couldn't control, in ways he hadn't anticipated. It had been a year since he had walked away from his life as Julian Westbrook, the heir to one of the wealthiest families in the country, and yet it felt like every shadow, every corner he turned, held something that reminded him of who he used to be. Every time he thought he was free, something tethered him to the past, pulling him back into the world he had abandoned.

It wasn't long before his suspicions were confirmed. The first sign came on a quiet Tuesday evening, just as the sun was beginning to dip below the horizon. Julian had been at Emily's café again, though he hadn't expected to see her that night. She had been avoiding him for the past few days, ever since the incident with the man in the café. Julian had no illusions—he knew he had overstepped. And he knew that the damage was done.

He had hoped that the evening would pass like any other, that he could slip into the shadows of the café and observe from a distance, just as he had done in the early days of his new life. But tonight, something felt different. There was a buzz in the air, a strange tension that made him feel more conspicuous than usual.

He had just taken his seat by the window when the door jingled, and a man walked in. Julian's gaze immediately snapped to him, an instinctive reaction. The man was tall, well-dressed in a suit that was just a bit too expensive for a café like this. His face was sharp, his eyes calculating, and as he scanned the room, Julian felt his pulse quicken. There was something about the way the man moved, the way he seemed to take everything in with one sweeping glance—it was the kind of arrogance that made Julian's skin crawl.

The man's gaze landed on the counter, and Julian followed his line of sight to Emily, who was standing behind it, arranging a tray of pastries. The man approached her with the kind of familiarity that set Julian's teeth on edge. It wasn't just that the man knew Emily, it was the way he moved toward her, as if he had every right to be there.

Emily glanced up, her expression unreadable, and Julian felt an inexplicable knot in his stomach. He had seen this before—the way men like this would enter a room, commanding attention, demanding respect. They had no qualms about pushing boundaries, about taking what they wanted.

But Emily's reaction was different. She wasn't smiling, she wasn't flirting, and most importantly, she wasn't engaging. She looked almost… apprehensive. Julian's eyes narrowed as the man leaned in just a little too close, speaking softly but with a tone that carried across the room. He couldn't hear the words, but the way Emily's posture stiffened, the way her hands trembled slightly as she wiped down the counter, told him everything he needed to know.

There was a moment of stillness—one that felt too long—and then Emily nodded, a forced, polite motion, before quickly turning away from the man. Julian watched as she stepped into the back room, her face hardening as she disappeared behind the kitchen door.

The man, however, didn't leave. He lingered at the counter, scanning the room as if he were waiting for something. Or someone.

Julian's instincts kicked into high gear. There was no way he could sit idly by and watch this unfold. Not after everything that had happened, not after the way things had shifted between him and Emily. His chest tightened, his fingers curled around the coffee cup in front of him as he weighed his options. What was it about this man that made him so uncomfortable? He had no idea, but one thing was certain—he wasn't about to let him get too close to Emily.

He stood up abruptly, his chair scraping against the floor as he made his way to the counter. As he approached, the man turned to him, his lips curling into a smirk.

"Is there a problem?" the man asked, his voice smooth, a hint of amusement in his tone.

Julian felt his jaw clench. He could feel his heart pounding in his chest, his pulse racing. There was something about the way the man looked at him—calculating, assessing—that sent a chill down his spine.

"No problem," Julian replied, forcing a smile. "Just wanted to make sure everything was alright."

The man raised an eyebrow. "Everything's fine. I was just having a conversation with your friend." His gaze flickered over Julian, then back to the door where Emily had disappeared. "But it seems like she's not interested in continuing it."

Julian didn't like the way the man was talking about Emily, as if she were some object to be discussed and dismissed. His fingers tightened around the counter, his nails digging into the wood as he fought to keep his composure.

"Well," Julian said, his voice deliberately calm, "I'm sure she'll appreciate your concern. But if you're done here, I'd suggest you leave." The words came out more harshly than he intended, and the man's smirk faltered for a moment.

"Is that so?" The man leaned in, his tone turning colder, more dangerous. "You don't know who I am, do you?"

Julian's stomach dropped. The words were a warning. He had heard them before. The man's demeanor shifted, his smile vanishing as he looked Julian up and down with a predatory gaze.

"I know exactly who you are," Julian said, his voice low, controlled. "And I think you'd do well to leave before this becomes a problem."

The man took a step back, his eyes flashing with something Julian couldn't quite place. But before he could say anything else, a voice broke through the tension.

"Is there a problem here?" Emily's voice was quiet, but firm. She had reappeared, standing just beyond the kitchen door, watching the two men with an unreadable expression. She was composed, but Julian could see the wariness in her eyes. She knew something was off.

The man straightened up, his expression hardening. "No problem," he said, a tight smile appearing on his face. "Just some old business. Nothing to worry about."

Emily looked between the two of them for a moment before nodding. "Good," she said softly, her eyes lingering on Julian before turning back to the man. "Now, if you're done, I'd appreciate it if you'd leave."

The man's jaw clenched, but he didn't argue. Instead, he turned on his heel and walked toward the door, his eyes flashing one last time in Julian's direction before he disappeared into the street. The bell above the door jingled as he left, and for a moment, Julian just stood there, trying to make sense of what had just happened.

Emily didn't speak at first. She didn't move, her gaze fixed on the door as if she were waiting for the man to come back. But when she finally turned to Julian, her expression was one of quiet resolve.

"Who was that?" Julian asked, his voice low, though he already knew the answer. He could feel the tension radiating off of her, the way her hands clenched into fists by her sides.

Emily shook her head, her jaw set. "Someone from my past," she said softly. "Someone I thought I was done with."

Julian felt a chill run through him. "What does he want?"

"He's not someone who takes no for an answer," Emily replied, her voice tight. "He's persistent. And dangerous."

Julian could feel his heart pounding in his chest. The weight of her words settled over him like a cloud, the implications of them far darker than anything he had imagined. The man wasn't just some random customer. He was a part of Emily's life—someone she had tried to escape. Someone from her past who had no intention of letting her go.

"What did you mean when you said you thought you were done with him?" Julian asked, his voice edged with urgency.

Emily hesitated for a moment, looking at him with a mixture of reluctance and trust. "He's part of the reason I left everything behind. I came here to get away from people like him. To start fresh."

Julian's stomach twisted. He had come to the café to escape his own past, and now he found himself tangled in someone else's. But it wasn't just about him anymore. Emily was in danger. And Julian wasn't going to let anyone from her past drag her back into a life she didn't want.

For the first time in a long time, Julian realized that his past wasn't the only one casting a shadow. Emily's was just as dark, just as dangerous.

And the man who had just left—he was only the beginning.

Seven

The Conflict Within

The weight of Emily's revelation hit Julian harder than he expected. She had tried to hide it, tried to keep it buried beneath the quiet hum of daily life, but it was impossible to ignore. The man she had been trying to escape, the one who had just walked into the café and threatened the fragile peace they had begun to build, was not just any past—he was a shadow, a nightmare that loomed over her life in ways Julian hadn't imagined.

His thoughts churned as he walked home that evening, the streets of the city growing darker with every step. He had been prepared for a lot of things in this new life of his—prepared for the awkwardness of pretending to be someone he wasn't, prepared for the struggle of leaving behind the wealth and privilege he had grown up with. But he hadn't been prepared for this. He hadn't been prepared to find himself entangled in

Emily's past, a past he knew nothing about and that she seemed determined to keep hidden from him.

The air felt colder now, the chill creeping under his jacket, but it wasn't the weather that made him shiver. It was the gnawing uncertainty that had taken root in his chest, the questions that had no answers. Was he really ready for this? Was he ready to be someone other than Julian Westbrook—the billionaire heir, the powerful man with everything at his disposal? Was he ready to be a man who had no wealth, no name, no status? A man who couldn't even be honest about his past to the woman he cared about?

He had thought he could walk away from everything. He had thought that by shedding his fortune, by stepping into the world of the ordinary, he would find something real. Something pure. But instead, he found himself stuck in the murky waters of his own lies, and now, with Emily's past crashing into the fragile walls he had built around himself, he was drowning.

He walked into his apartment, slamming the door behind him as the tension in his shoulders broke. The place was silent, the same stark, impersonal space it had been since he'd moved in. There was nothing here to anchor him, nothing to distract him from the chaos in his mind. He needed answers. He needed to understand what Emily had been through and how, after everything, he could protect her. But more than that, he needed to understand himself—why he had stayed in this life, why he had chosen to hide from the truth.

He walked to the window and stared out at the skyline, the lights of the city flickering like distant stars. His fingers traced the cool glass as he thought about Emily, about her quiet strength, her unwillingness to let anyone get too close. He understood that now. She had been protecting herself, just as he had. But she wasn't the only one who had secrets. He had his own, and they were starting to catch up with him in ways he couldn't control.

A knock at the door startled him from his thoughts, and Julian froze. He wasn't expecting anyone, not tonight. His pulse quickened, and for a moment, he considered ignoring it. But he couldn't. Not after the confrontation with Emily earlier. He needed to know where things stood between them. He needed to understand if there was still a chance, or if the past—his past, her past—was too much for either of them to overcome.

He opened the door slowly, his breath catching in his throat when he saw who was standing there.

Emily.

Her expression was unreadable, her face pale, her eyes shadowed with something he couldn't name. She looked exhausted, as though she had been carrying something heavy for a long time. The sight of her—standing there in front of him, looking so vulnerable—made his chest tighten, and for a moment, he didn't know what to say.

"Can we talk?" she asked, her voice barely above a whisper.

Julian stepped aside, motioning for her to come in. "Of course," he said, his voice strained.

Emily walked past him, her steps slow and deliberate. She didn't look at him as she passed, and Julian could feel the space between them widening with each second that ticked by. It wasn't just the physical distance—it was something deeper, something he couldn't ignore. They were both standing on the edge of a precipice, and the only question was whether they would jump together or fall apart.

He closed the door behind them, and for a long moment, neither of them spoke. The silence stretched on, thick with the weight of everything they hadn't said. Finally, Emily broke the stillness, her voice trembling slightly.

"I didn't want you to get involved," she said, her back turned to him as she spoke. "I didn't want to drag you into my mess. You deserve better than that."

Julian frowned. "Emily, you didn't drag me into anything. I chose this. I chose you."

She turned then, her eyes meeting his. There was a rawness in her gaze, a vulnerability that made Julian's heart ache. "But you didn't know what you were choosing," she said softly. "You didn't know the kind of person I was, the things I've been through. And now you do. I never meant for you to see that side of me."

Julian stepped closer, his voice low. "You don't have to explain yourself to me. You don't have to carry that weight alone."

But Emily shook her head, her eyes brimming with unshed tears. "I'm not the person you think I am, Julian. I'm not the woman you've been coming here to see every day. I've been hiding who I am for so long that I don't even know how to let anyone in anymore."

Julian's heart clenched. "I don't care about your past, Emily. I care about you. What matters to me is who you are now, and what you want."

She took a deep breath, her eyes closing for a moment as if gathering the strength to say the words. When she opened them again, there was a flicker of something—something he couldn't quite place—but it was there, in the way her lips parted as if she were about to tell him something important.

"I wish it were that simple," she whispered. "But there's more to it than just me. There's him."

Julian's pulse skipped a beat. "Who?"

She looked down, her hands shaking slightly. "Darren. He's the one I've been running from. The one who never lets go."

The name hit Julian like a cold wave. He had heard it before, in passing, but never like this. Darren was the man who had come into the café that day, the one whose very presence had made Julian's skin crawl. But now, hearing Emily say his name, hearing the fear in her voice, Julian knew that Darren wasn't just some past lover or a random acquaintance. He was a threat—a threat that had followed Emily to this place, to this life she had fought so hard to build.

"Who is he, Emily?" Julian's voice was urgent now, desperate for answers. "Why is he so dangerous?"

She hesitated for a moment, and when she spoke again, her words were laced with regret. "He's my ex. But he's more than that. He's manipulative, controlling. He has a way of getting into your head, making you believe things that aren't true. I thought I could escape him, that moving to this city would be enough. But now, he's found me again."

Julian's mind raced. He thought about everything she had just said—about the way Darren had looked at her in the café, the way he had been too close, too familiar. Julian had sensed the danger the moment he had seen him. And now, it seemed like that danger was too real, too close.

"I won't let him hurt you," Julian said, his voice fierce, filled with a determination he hadn't known he had.

Emily shook her head, her voice breaking. "It's not that simple, Julian. He doesn't just go away. He doesn't let go. And when he wants something, he'll do whatever it takes to get it."

Julian's thoughts were a whirlwind, but one thing was clear: he couldn't stand by and let Emily face this alone. He had to protect her, no matter what it cost him. But as the gravity of her words sank in, a deep fear gripped him. He was already in too deep. He had crossed a line he couldn't uncross. He had chosen to step into Emily's world, and now he couldn't walk away.

But there was something else, something that made his chest tighten with uncertainty: he had been lying to her. He had been lying to himself. What would happen when the truth about who he was finally came out? Could Emily ever accept the truth about him, about his past, when her own was threatening to consume her?

The conflict raged within him, but as he looked at Emily—broken, vulnerable, yet still strong in her own way—he knew one thing for certain: he wasn't walking away. Not now. Not ever.

"I'm not going anywhere," Julian said, his voice steady. "We'll face this together. All of it."

Emily looked at him, her eyes filled with a mixture of relief and fear. And in that moment, Julian knew that nothing would ever be the same again. The past was coming for both of them, and they would have to fight it together, or it would destroy them both.

Eight

The Moment of Betrayal

Julian hadn't expected it to happen like this. In his mind, he had prepared himself for everything—confronting Darren, protecting Emily, facing the fallout of his own lies—but he had never imagined that the betrayal would come from someone so close, someone he thought he could trust without question.

It started like any other day. Emily had agreed to meet him at a small café on the other side of town, away from the familiar corners of the café they had frequented together. The evening air was crisp, a light breeze stirring the autumn leaves scattered across the sidewalks. Julian had arrived early, as usual, his heart pounding with the weight of their situation. Since their conversation the night before, things had felt more fragile, more precarious. He had vowed to protect Emily from Darren, to stand by her through whatever came next, but he couldn't ignore the nagging fear that had taken root deep in his chest. He didn't know how long he could keep pretending. How long he could keep up the act of being someone he wasn't, just to be with her.

The truth was, he had never imagined his own past would become a weapon against him. He had hoped that Emily would accept him for who he was in the present—not the man who had come from wealth, not the man who had so desperately run away from his former life. But there it was, gnawing at him—his past was a ticking time bomb, and sooner or later, it would go off. He just didn't know when, or how. But he knew one thing: Emily deserved the truth, all of it, no matter how painful it might be.

He glanced at his watch. She was late—later than usual. Julian shifted uncomfortably in his seat, the pressure of the situation weighing heavily on his shoulders. It wasn't just about Darren anymore. The walls were closing in on him from all sides. Emily was distancing herself, and Julian couldn't tell if it was because of his actions or the secret that had been hanging between them. Every day, it felt like something was slipping away.

After another ten minutes of staring at the door, Julian decided to call her. He pulled out his phone, dialing her number. It rang three times before going to voicemail. He stared at the screen, a knot tightening in his stomach. She had been distant lately, but this felt different.

Just as he was about to leave a message, his phone vibrated in his hand. A new message appeared, but it wasn't from Emily. It was a number he didn't recognize. His pulse quickened as he opened the message, his breath catching when he read the first line.

"I know who you really are."

Julian's heart skipped a beat, and a cold sweat prickled at his skin. The message continued.

"You can't hide from your past forever. I'm giving you one chance to come clean to her. Tell Emily the truth before I do."

The message was signed with a single initial: D.

Julian's mind raced. Darren. Of course. He had been waiting for this moment, waiting for the inevitable confrontation. But it wasn't just about the past anymore; it was about Emily. About their future. And now, Darren was playing his hand, forcing Julian's hand in a way he hadn't anticipated. He had warned him before. He had threatened him with the consequences of his actions. But Julian had underestimated him. Darren wasn't just a shadow from Emily's past. He was a threat, a constant presence lurking just outside the perimeter of their lives, waiting to tear everything down.

The door to the café opened, and Julian looked up, his breath catching in his throat. Emily stepped inside, her eyes scanning the room, her expression unreadable. For a moment, their gazes locked, but it wasn't the familiar warmth he had come to expect. There was something in her eyes, something colder, something more guarded.

Julian stood up, his pulse racing. He opened his mouth to speak, but the words stuck in his throat. He didn't know where to begin. The truth? The lies? The choices he had made? He had spent so much time keeping secrets from her, afraid of losing her, but now it seemed like he was losing her anyway.

"Emily," he said, his voice tight. "I'm glad you came. I was worried—"

"You should be," she interrupted, her voice calm but firm. She didn't smile. She didn't make small talk. Instead, she walked toward the table with purpose, sitting down across from him without waiting for him to invite her.

Julian's heart thudded painfully in his chest. "What's going on? Is everything okay?"

Emily looked at him for a long moment, her expression still unreadable, before she finally spoke. "I don't know what's going on, Julian. I don't know if I can trust you anymore."

The words hit him like a slap, knocking the breath out of him. His world tilted, spinning on its axis. "What do you mean?"

She didn't respond right away. Instead, she reached into her bag and pulled out her phone. She slid it across the table toward him, the screen facing up. Julian's heart sank as he looked down at the message displayed in front of him.

"I know who you really are."

The words were a cruel reminder of the truth he had tried so hard to bury. He swallowed hard, his throat tight with guilt. "Emily, I—"

She held up her hand, stopping him before he could speak. "No. Don't say anything yet. I need to hear it from you. I need to hear you tell me the truth."

Julian's mind went blank for a moment, a thousand thoughts crashing together in a dizzying storm. How could he explain this? How could he tell her everything now, when it felt like everything had already fallen apart? He could hear Darren's words echoing in his mind—"Tell her the truth before I do."

"I never meant for you to find out like this," Julian said, his voice cracking as he finally met her eyes. "I didn't want to hide this from you, but I… I didn't know how to tell you. I didn't want to lose you."

Emily's gaze never wavered. "Tell me, then. Tell me who you really are. Tell me what you've been hiding from me all this time."

Julian took a deep breath, trying to steady his shaking hands. "I'm Julian Westbrook. I'm the heir to Westbrook Enterprises. I was born into wealth and power, and I ran away from it. I gave it all up to start over. To be someone different. I thought if I could get away from that life, I could find something real. But I didn't expect it to hurt like this."

Emily didn't say anything for a long time. She just stared at him, her expression unreadable, and Julian could feel the weight of her silence crushing him from all sides.

"You lied to me," she finally said, her voice barely above a whisper.

"I didn't want to lie," Julian pleaded. "I wanted to be honest with you, but I didn't know how. I didn't know if you would still love me if you knew the truth. So I ran from it. But I can't keep running, Emily. Not anymore."

"Do you think I'm stupid?" Emily's voice was cold now, the warmth she had once offered him gone. "Do you think I wouldn't notice? Do you think I wouldn't find out eventually?"

"Emily, please, let me explain—"

"No, Julian," she cut him off, her eyes flashing with a mix of hurt and anger. "You don't get to explain. You don't get to lie to me and then expect everything to be okay. This isn't some game, some little secret you get to keep hidden until it's convenient for you to tell me. This is my life, and I thought I could trust you."

Julian's heart shattered. He had never felt this small, this powerless. He had been so consumed with his own fear, his own insecurities, that he hadn't stopped to consider the consequences of his actions. He had hurt the one person he cared about more than anything, and he didn't know how to fix it.

"Emily, I never meant to hurt you," he whispered, his voice raw with emotion. "I thought I could keep this secret, keep us safe, but I was wrong. I was selfish, and I'm sorry."

Emily stood up abruptly, her chair scraping against the floor. "I need to go," she said, her voice shaking with barely contained rage. "I can't do this anymore. I can't keep pretending that everything is fine when I know you've been lying to me."

"Emily, please," Julian begged, standing up as well, reaching out for her. "Don't leave like this. Please, just give me a chance to make it right."

But she pulled away, her eyes filled with tears. "You've already made your choice, Julian. And I've made mine."

Without another word, she turned and walked out of the café, leaving Julian standing there, alone. The moment of betrayal had come, and now, all that was left was the wreckage of the life he had tried to build—a life that had been torn apart by his own lies.

As Julian stood there, his heart breaking, he realized one painful truth: the price of betrayal was far higher than he had ever imagined.

Nine

The Truth Hurts

The rain had started falling in sheets, heavy and relentless, by the time Julian left the café. It came down in torrents, drenching the streets and the world around him, but it was nothing compared to the storm inside his chest. His feet moved mechanically, as if the force of the rain might drown out the relentless barrage of thoughts hammering away inside his mind. He barely noticed the people rushing past him, the occasional car splashing through the puddles, or the distant sounds of the city in the throes of the evening.

All he could think about was Emily—her face, her eyes, the cold distance she had shown him. The betrayal had cut deeper than anything he had ever imagined. He had never anticipated that revealing the truth would cost him everything. But in the end, he realized that he hadn't just lied to her about who he was. He had lied to himself about how much he could control, how much he could hide from the past.

He hadn't been prepared for the look in her eyes when she left. The betrayal in her gaze was so sharp, so final, that it felt like a physical blow. Emily had trusted him, and in the end, he had broken that trust. Not just once, but with every day he had kept the truth from her. He had built a life on secrets, and in the end, those secrets had come crashing down around him.

Julian's thoughts spiraled as he made his way back to his apartment. The streets were a blur as he walked through them, his mind replaying their conversation over and over again. Her voice had been cold, her words like ice. She had every right to be angry, every right to feel betrayed, but it didn't stop the crushing weight of guilt from suffocating him.

I thought I could keep this secret, keep us safe, but I was wrong.

The words echoed in his mind, a constant reminder of how badly he had misjudged everything. He hadn't thought about the consequences of hiding the truth. He hadn't thought about the impact it would have on her, on their relationship. In his desperation to be someone else, someone free from his past, he had lost the only thing that mattered. He had lost her.

The door to his apartment clicked shut behind him, and he stood there for a long moment, staring at the dark, empty space before him. The weight of the silence in the room felt oppressive, like the walls themselves were closing in on him. He had never felt more alone.

The Truth Hurts

The sound of his phone vibrating on the table broke through the stillness, but he didn't move. He couldn't bring himself to look at it. He already knew it was Emily. The message would be just as cold, just as final as the look she had given him when she walked out. He didn't need to see it to know what it would say.

But the phone buzzed again, and this time, he couldn't ignore it. With a heavy sigh, Julian reached for it and unlocked the screen.

It was a message from a number he didn't recognize.

"I know what you've done."

His heart skipped a beat as his thumb hovered over the screen. The words were simple, direct—but it was the chilling implication behind them that made Julian's stomach churn. He had no idea who the message was from, but it sent a wave of dread crashing over him. He wasn't prepared for this. He wasn't ready for whatever this person was about to reveal.

The message continued.

"I know who you really are. And if you don't do what I say, I'll make sure Emily finds out everything. The truth you've been hiding, the lies you've told. It'll all come crashing down. This is your last chance."

Julian felt his blood run cold. He didn't have to ask who it was. He knew. The message had Darren's fingerprints all over it.

The tone, the threat—it was unmistakable. Darren had always been a master of control, of manipulation. And now, he was making it clear that he had more power over Julian's life than Julian had realized.

Tell Emily the truth before I do, Darren had warned him. And now, Darren had made good on that threat, using the very thing Julian had worked so hard to bury against him.

Julian's hands clenched into fists, his mind racing with a thousand thoughts, none of them clear. He couldn't let this happen. He couldn't let Darren destroy everything. But how could he fix it? How could he undo the damage he had already done?

The storm outside intensified, thunder rumbling through the night as though the heavens themselves were reflecting the chaos inside Julian's mind. He had tried to control the narrative, tried to hold onto some semblance of his past, but now everything was slipping away from him. Everything he had tried to protect, everything he had fought for, was unraveling before his eyes.

His phone buzzed again, this time with a call from Emily. Julian hesitated, his heart pounding. He knew he should answer. He knew he needed to try and explain, to tell her the truth—his truth—but the weight of her anger, of her disappointment, was more than he could bear. What could he say to her now? What words could undo the damage he had done?

The phone stopped ringing, and Julian let out a long breath.

The Truth Hurts

The silence that followed felt suffocating. He needed to act. He needed to make a choice. The truth, no matter how painful, was the only way forward. If he didn't tell her, if he didn't come clean, he would lose her for good. But how could he find the courage to do it? How could he bear the weight of the words he needed to say?

He grabbed his coat from the hook by the door, his fingers trembling as he put it on. The rain outside had turned into a steady downpour, but it didn't matter. He had to see her. He had to make things right, or at least try. He couldn't keep running from the truth. It was time to face it.

The streets were nearly deserted as he walked toward Emily's apartment. The sound of the rain pounding against the pavement was deafening, but it did little to drown out the thoughts that consumed him. He had spent so long hiding from the truth that he had forgotten what it meant to be honest. He had built walls around himself, convinced that they would protect him from the world. But now, those walls were crumbling, and all that was left was the raw, painful truth.

Julian reached the building where Emily lived, his heart hammering in his chest as he stood outside, staring up at her window. He had no idea what to expect when he saw her, no idea how she would react. But one thing was certain—he couldn't hide anymore. The truth had already begun to unravel, and he had no choice but to face it.

He pressed the buzzer, his finger lingering for a moment before releasing it. The door clicked open, and Julian stepped inside, the familiar warmth of the building doing little to ease the tension in his chest. As he made his way up the stairs, every step felt heavier than the last. He had come this far, but he wasn't sure he was ready for what was about to happen. Was he ready to lose her? To face the consequences of his lies?

When he reached her door, he hesitated. He could hear the faint sound of movement inside, the soft shuffle of feet on the floor. Julian took a deep breath, gathering whatever courage he had left, and knocked. The sound echoed in the hallway, a hollow reminder of everything that was at stake.

The door opened slowly, and Emily stood there, her expression guarded, her eyes red from crying. She looked at him for a long moment, her gaze unreadable.

"You came," she said, her voice soft, almost resigned.

"I had to," Julian replied, his voice barely above a whisper. "I'm sorry, Emily. I should've told you the truth from the start. But I didn't know how. I didn't know how to explain everything without losing you. And now, I've lost you anyway."

Emily's lips trembled, but she didn't speak. She stepped back, letting him into the apartment, but there was no warmth in her gesture, no welcome. The walls between them were higher than ever, and Julian could feel the distance in every inch of space that separated them.

"I know I've hurt you," he said, his voice breaking. "I've lied to you. I've kept so much from you, and I'm sorry. I never meant

The Truth Hurts

for it to be like this. I thought I could protect you from the truth. But the truth always hurts, doesn't it? No matter how hard we try to avoid it."

Emily didn't answer. She simply stood there, her eyes locked on him, the silence stretching between them like a chasm too wide to cross. And in that moment, Julian realized that no matter how hard he tried, no matter how much he wanted to fix things, the truth had already done its damage.

The truth hurt. And now, there was no escaping it.

Ten

The Wall Between Them

T he apartment felt colder than it ever had before. Julian stepped inside, his shoes heavy on the wooden floor, each step echoing with a finality he couldn't escape. The door clicked shut behind him, but the sound was muffled, as though the walls of Emily's small, intimate space had swallowed the noise, leaving only silence between them.

She didn't invite him in, but she didn't tell him to leave either. She merely stepped back, her eyes betraying nothing but an unreadable coldness that settled like a thick fog in the room. Emily stood near the window, arms crossed, looking out at the rain that had yet to stop. The view was familiar, one Julian had seen a hundred times before from the same position. But tonight, it was different. Tonight, everything felt distant, as though the rain was not just a storm outside, but the separation that had bloomed between them, filling the space with a suffocating pressure.

"Emily," Julian started, his voice rough, his hands shaking slightly at his sides. He had come here to fix things, to break down the walls that had sprung up between them. But now that he was here, he didn't know how to begin. He could feel the weight of her silence, feel it pressing against him, and it was all he could do to stand there without crumbling under the pressure.

Emily didn't turn around immediately. She stood there for a long moment, staring out into the night as though the city below could offer her the answers that neither of them could provide. Finally, her voice broke the stillness, low and steady, but filled with something deeper—a bitterness that Julian hadn't expected.

"Why didn't you tell me, Julian? Why didn't you just tell me who you were from the beginning?" Her back was still to him, her shoulders tense, but her words carried a weight that seemed to fill the room.

Julian felt his throat tighten, as though the very question she was asking was one he had been choking on for weeks. The truth had been building inside him, pushing against his ribs, trying to break free, but he had kept it contained, hidden behind lies and half-truths, because he thought that if he could just keep her in the dark, it would all work out. But now, as her words cut through the air, he realized just how far from the truth he had been.

"I didn't want to lose you, Emily," he said quietly, his voice hoarse. "I thought if you knew who I really was, what I really came from, it would change everything between us. I thought you'd see me differently, and not in the way I wanted you to. I thought if I kept pretending to be someone else, we could have something real. But it was all a lie."

Emily's body stiffened at his confession. She didn't turn to face him, but Julian could feel the tension in the room, could sense the invisible wall that had started to rise between them the moment his words left his mouth. She was silent for a long time, her breathing shallow, as though she were holding her emotions back, trying to decide what to say or whether she should say anything at all. Julian's heart beat faster, thumping against his chest like a prisoner trying to break free.

But then, without warning, Emily spoke again, and her words hit him like a slap. "A lie?" she repeated softly, her voice carrying a dangerous edge that Julian hadn't heard before. "That's what this all was to you? A lie? I'm just some... experiment? Some 'real thing' that you could 'have,' as if I'm some kind of prize you could win by being someone else?"

Julian recoiled, the accusation striking deep. He hadn't thought of it that way, hadn't realized how cold his actions must have seemed, how they must have felt to her. The very thing he had tried so hard to escape—his wealth, his status, the label of who he was—had now been used against him in a way he never intended.

"No," he said, shaking his head, his voice rising in desperation.

"It wasn't like that. You're not an experiment, Emily. You're—" He stopped, his words catching in his throat. "I didn't want you to see me as that person. As the man I used to be. I just wanted you to see the real me. The man who wanted to be with you."

Emily's eyes, still fixed on the rain outside, shimmered with something Julian couldn't quite identify. But whatever it was, it was cold—ice cold, a stark contrast to the warmth she had once shared with him. She finally turned around, and Julian saw the tears brimming in her eyes. But they weren't the tears of vulnerability he had once seen in her, the ones that had made him want to protect her. No, these were the tears of betrayal, the kind that cut deep, leaving scars that would take a lifetime to heal, if they ever healed at all.

"You think you're the only one who's lied, Julian?" Emily asked, her voice quiet, but thick with anger and hurt. "You think I haven't been lying to you too? You think I haven't kept things from you? My past... the things I've been running from? The things that made me leave everything behind just to come here, to try to be something else, someone else? You think I haven't been hiding from you just as much as you've been hiding from me?"

Her words hit him harder than any blow he could have received. Julian's chest tightened as the realization hit him: they were both running from their own truths. They had both constructed lives built on deception, trying to escape parts of themselves that they didn't know how to accept. He had run from his wealth and privilege, and Emily had run from a past that she couldn't bear to confront. They had both thought they could find something pure, something real, in a life that was built on nothing but pretenses.

But now, with the truth laid bare between them, Julian realized how much they had both lost. They had both been lying to each other, and now there was a wall between them, a wall built on guilt, on mistrust, on the deep knowledge that everything they had shared up until now had been tainted by the lies they had told.

"I'm not proud of my past, Julian," Emily whispered, her voice trembling. "But I thought I could leave it behind. I thought I could start over. But it's all catching up to me. It's all catching up to us."

The words hung in the air between them, thick with the weight of the truth. Julian stood there, his body rigid, unsure of what to do, unsure of what to say. He had come here to fix things, to break down the walls between them, but now, he wasn't sure that was even possible. The damage had been done, and no amount of apologizing, no amount of explaining, could change what had already been set in motion.

"I didn't want to hurt you, Emily," Julian said softly, his voice breaking. "I never wanted to hurt you. But I've hurt you more than I could ever explain. And now, I don't know how to fix it."

Emily's expression softened slightly, but the coldness was still there, lurking beneath the surface. "I don't know how to trust you anymore, Julian. I don't know if I can."

The words were like a dagger to his heart, but they were the truth. The hardest truth he had ever had to face. Trust had been the foundation of everything they had built together, and now, that foundation was cracked, shattered by the lies they had both told. He had lost her trust, and no amount of pleading could rebuild what had been broken.

"Maybe we need time," Julian whispered, his voice barely audible. "Maybe we need time to figure this out. I'll do whatever it takes. Whatever you need."

But Emily shook her head, her eyes distant. "Time isn't going to fix this. Time isn't going to erase the lies. Time isn't going to bring back the trust we've lost."

Julian felt the air in the room grow colder, the space between them expanding with every passing second. The silence that followed was deafening, the kind of silence that spoke volumes, the kind that marked the end of something that had once been beautiful.

And in that silence, Julian knew—there was no easy way back from this. No simple solution, no magical fix. The truth had been laid bare, and now, there was nothing left but the weight of the consequences.

The wall between them had been built, brick by brick, from the lies they had told, the secrets they had kept. And as much as he wished he could tear it down, as much as he wanted to reach out to her, he knew deep down that it would take more than words, more than promises, to ever make things right again.

For now, all he could do was stand there, on the other side of that wall, watching as Emily turned away from him once more, the space between them growing wider with each passing second.

And in the silence, he realized that sometimes the truth didn't set you free. Sometimes, the truth only made everything worse.

Eleven

The Redemption Road

The days following their confrontation felt like an endless blur to Julian. The silence between him and Emily had only deepened, the chasm between them widening with every unspoken word, every moment that passed in awkward, painful stillness. Julian had tried to reach out—texts, calls, visits—but Emily was resolute. Each time, she put up a barrier, one more layer of ice between them, as if she were trying to protect herself from the storm that had ravaged what they had once shared.

But the more Julian tried, the more he realized something that had been gnawing at him from the start: this was not something he could fix overnight. The damage had been done, and no amount of apologies or heartfelt confessions would erase the hurt he had caused. The walls he had built around himself were crumbling, and now, they stood between him and the only person who mattered.

The cold truth had set in. He had lied to her, not just once but repeatedly. He had kept secrets, buried parts of himself so deep that even he had started to believe they didn't matter. But now, in the wake of everything that had happened, those lies hung over him like a dark cloud. The truth had finally come out, but instead of feeling free, he felt more trapped than ever. The one person he wanted to be with, the one person who had made him feel like he could start over, now seemed like a distant memory, someone locked behind a door he couldn't reach.

The rain had stopped, but the grey clouds still hung heavily in the sky, casting the world in a muted, melancholic light. Julian sat at the kitchen table in his sparse apartment, staring at the cup of coffee in front of him, watching the steam rise from the surface. He had no answers, no clear path forward. The weight of the uncertainty felt suffocating, but there was something else stirring in him now. A quiet resolve, a flicker of determination that he hadn't felt in a long time.

He knew that he had to do something. He couldn't just sit here and let everything slip away. If he was ever going to make things right, it was going to take more than regret. It was going to take action. The lies he had told, the walls he had built, were his doing, and it was time to take responsibility for them. He had to prove to Emily that he was more than the man who had run from the truth. He had to show her that he could be someone who faced the consequences of his actions and worked to make amends.

But where to start? What could he possibly do to fix the mess he had created?

His phone buzzed on the table, snapping him from his thoughts. Julian picked it up, hesitated, then swiped it open. A message from an unknown number.

"I've given you a chance. I hope you don't waste it."

Julian's stomach tightened as he read the words. Darren. The threat he had made was still hanging over him, a constant reminder of how far Julian's past could reach, how much control Darren had over his life, no matter how far he tried to run from it. This wasn't just about Emily anymore. This was about everything—the life he had tried to escape, the life he had been born into, the people who wouldn't let him go.

For a moment, Julian considered ignoring the message. He could delete it, block the number, pretend it didn't matter. But that was the problem, wasn't it? Pretending. Hiding. Running from the truth. He had been doing it for so long, and now, it was time to face the reality of it all. He had to face Darren. He had to face his past, no matter how painful it was.

With a deep breath, Julian typed out a quick response.

"I'm done running. You'll get nothing from me."

He hit send before he could second-guess himself. The moment the words left his phone, he felt a weight lift from his shoulders, but he knew this was just the beginning. The road to redemption wasn't going to be easy, and he was just taking the first step.

Julian stood up and walked to the window, watching the city below. It was a familiar view, one that had once made him feel invincible, like he could conquer the world. But now, it felt distant, almost alien. He had built his life on falsehoods, and now the very city that had given him everything felt empty.

But maybe that was the point. Maybe, in order to rebuild, he had to start with nothing. He had to strip away everything he had been hiding behind, every layer of deception, and face the person he had become.

His thoughts turned to Emily, as they always did. He had hurt her. And he knew that no amount of words would undo that pain. But he also knew that he couldn't give up. He couldn't walk away from her now. He had to show her that he could change. He had to prove to her that he was worthy of her trust again.

It was a long road ahead, one that was fraught with obstacles and setbacks. But Julian knew that if he was ever going to find redemption, it would have to be through action, not words. He had to show Emily that he wasn't the same man he had been when they first met. He had to prove that he could stand up for the truth, even when it hurt.

The next day, Julian found himself at the same café where it had all started, standing outside in front of the door, unsure of what he was about to do. He had thought about this moment for days, and yet now that he was here, he felt the weight of his own indecision. What could he say to her that would make things right? How could he possibly explain everything he had been running from?

But he couldn't let fear stop him. He had made mistakes, but he was done hiding from them. He pushed open the door and walked inside, his heart pounding as he scanned the room for her. The familiar smell of coffee and pastries filled the air, but it was the absence of Emily that hit him first. She wasn't behind the counter, and the café felt empty without her presence.

A pang of disappointment shot through him, but he pushed it aside. He had come here to find her, to make things right, not to give up. He glanced around the café, his eyes searching for any sign of her, when a voice broke through the silence.

"You're here early."

Julian turned around, and there she was. Emily. Standing in the doorway to the back room, her eyes wide with surprise. She wasn't smiling, but she wasn't angry either. There was something different in her expression—uncertainty, maybe, but also a flicker of hope.

"I didn't expect you to come back," Emily said, her voice quiet, but not cold. "I thought... I thought you might be done."

Julian took a step toward her, his heart racing. "I'm not done," he said, his voice steady but full of emotion. "I've hurt you, Emily. I've lied to you. I've kept so much from you, and I know

I don't deserve your forgiveness. But I'm not running anymore. I'm here to face the truth. All of it."

Emily didn't respond right away, but she didn't look away either. She simply stood there, watching him, waiting.

"I know it's going to take more than words," Julian continued, his chest tight. "But I'm ready to do whatever it takes to make things right. I can't change the past, but I can be honest with you now. I can prove to you that I'm not the man I used to be."

Her gaze softened, just for a moment, but it was enough to make Julian feel like he was standing on solid ground for the first time in days.

"I don't know what happens next, Julian," Emily said, her voice low, uncertain. "I don't know if I can trust you again. But I'm willing to listen. I'm willing to see if we can start over. Together. But only if you're ready to do the work. Only if you're ready to face the truth, no matter how painful it is."

Julian nodded, his throat tight with emotion. "I'm ready. I'll do whatever it takes."

For the first time in what felt like forever, Emily took a step toward him, her eyes searching his, weighing his sincerity. "Then we take it one step at a time. We rebuild from the ground up."

Julian's heart lifted at her words, the weight that had been pressing on him for so long lifting just a little. He didn't know what the future held, but he knew that he had to take that first step. The road to redemption was long and uncertain, but for the first time, Julian believed that it was a road worth walking.

With Emily standing before him, with the possibility of something real, he knew that the journey ahead—no matter how difficult—was one he was ready to take.

The redemption road had begun.

Twelve

The Hidden Agenda

The café was quieter than usual that morning, the gentle hum of conversation muted as if the world had decided to hold its breath. Julian sat at his usual table by the window, his coffee cooling in front of him, but his thoughts were far from the warmth of the cup. His fingers drummed absentmindedly on the rim, the rhythm of his nervousness punctuating the silence.

It had been two weeks since his last conversation with Emily. Two weeks since he had finally confronted the truth, faced the lies he had told, and made the decision to be someone better, someone who was worthy of her trust. The air between them had changed since that day. The walls had come down, but only slightly. He could feel the tentative steps they were both taking toward rebuilding what had once been. There was no rush—just a fragile, quiet progress that was more healing than anything else.

But there was still something in the back of his mind, a gnawing feeling that wouldn't go away. The message from Darren still lingered, echoing in his thoughts. It hadn't been a threat so much as a challenge, an ultimatum that Julian couldn't ignore. Darren's power over his past wasn't something he could simply wish away. And with each day that passed, Julian felt the weight of his own decisions growing heavier.

Emily had no idea what he was still up against—what he was still running from. She had only seen the man he had become, not the man he had been. And while they were building something new between them, there were pieces of Julian's past that wouldn't stay buried, no matter how hard he tried to keep them locked away.

The bell above the café door jingled, and Julian looked up, his thoughts breaking as his gaze found Emily. She walked toward him with a hesitant smile, her eyes cautious but warmer than the last time he had seen her. She was wearing the same blue sweater she'd worn the first time they had met in the café, and as she approached, Julian couldn't help but feel the weight of how far they had come since that day. But there was something in the way she looked at him now—a wariness—that hadn't been there before.

"Hey," she said softly, her voice still tinged with uncertainty. She slid into the chair opposite him, her movements deliberate, as if she were testing the waters between them. "How's your morning?"

"Same as usual," Julian replied, his smile faint but genuine. "Busy. But... good."

Emily nodded, her gaze flickering between him and the door, as if she were expecting something—or someone—to show up at any moment. Julian noticed the subtle tension in her posture, the way her fingers fiddled with the edge of her cup. It wasn't like her to be so restless.

"You okay?" he asked, leaning forward slightly, concern bubbling in his chest.

Emily hesitated for a moment before meeting his eyes, her expression unreadable. "I'm fine. Just... I've been thinking a lot about everything lately."

Julian's stomach tightened. He knew this conversation was coming. He had known from the moment they had started to rebuild their connection that there would be a moment when everything would come to a head, when the walls they had built would crack open, and the reality of their situation would come pouring out.

"About us?" he asked carefully, trying not to sound too eager or too desperate. The truth was, every word she spoke had become a weight on his chest, because every word meant something—something that could either bring them closer or push them further apart.

Emily nodded, her eyes softening. "About... trust. About what we're building here, Julian."

His heart skipped a beat. "And what are we building?"

She let out a sigh, looking down at her coffee cup. "I don't know yet. But… I want to believe in it. I want to believe in us. But there's something—something I still don't know. And I think you're hiding something from me."

Julian's breath caught in his throat, a cold sweat breaking out across his back. She wasn't angry. She wasn't accusing him. But she was asking questions, probing for answers that he didn't have, and his instinct was to retreat, to run from the past he had been so carefully concealing.

"I'm not hiding anything, Emily," he said quickly, his voice betraying him slightly, but he forced himself to meet her gaze. "I swear, I'm not."

But even as the words left his mouth, Julian felt the weight of his own deceit. He wasn't lying about his feelings for her—those were real, deep, and true—but there was still so much she didn't know. So much he hadn't told her about the choices he had made, the people he had crossed, the ties that bound him to a life he could never escape.

Emily seemed to search his face for a moment, her gaze steady, before she spoke again. "I've been thinking a lot about that day—the day I found out about your past. I think I understand why you didn't want to tell me, Julian. But I need to know… I need to know if there's anything else you're keeping from me. Because I can't keep building something with someone who's hiding parts of themselves. I just can't."

Julian swallowed hard. The air between them was heavy now, thick with the weight of her words. This wasn't just about them anymore. This was about his past. And for the first time in days, the shadow of Darren's threat loomed large again, a dark presence in the corner of his mind.

"You're right," he said slowly, his voice barely above a whisper. "There is something else. But it's not just about me anymore, Emily. It's about us, and about the things I've been running from. Things that, if you knew... I don't think you'd want anything to do with me."

The words felt like they had been waiting to break free, like a dam finally cracking under the pressure. Emily's eyes softened, and she reached across the table, her hand brushing lightly against his.

"Julian, I told you that I want to be here, that I want to build something with you. But I can't do that if you keep shutting me out. If you keep me in the dark about things that matter. Whatever it is—whatever it involves—I can handle it. I just need you to trust me."

The sincerity in her voice made his heart ache, but the truth that was coming—he could feel it building inside him, pushing him forward—was too big to ignore anymore. It was time to tell her. All of it.

Before he could speak, the door to the café opened again, and the moment was broken. Julian turned to see a man step inside, tall and broad-shouldered, wearing an expensive suit that screamed power. The man's eyes immediately found Julian's, and for a split second, everything stopped. The room grew still, the noise of the café fading into the background. Julian's heart skipped a beat, and a cold chill swept over him.

It was Darren.

Julian's stomach dropped. Emily's hand, still on his, froze as well. She looked up at him, confusion flickering in her eyes before she turned to look at the man who had just walked in.

Darren's smile was tight, a predatory grin that made Julian's skin crawl. He didn't say a word to anyone else in the room as he made his way toward their table, his eyes fixed on Julian like a predator stalking its prey.

"Didn't expect to see you here, Julian," Darren said, his voice smooth, dripping with mock friendliness. "I thought I'd find you hiding, somewhere where I couldn't get to you. But you've been making a lot of noise lately. Haven't you?"

Julian stood up, his fists clenched at his sides. He could feel the tension in the air, the weight of the past bearing down on him. Emily looked between them, her confusion deepening with every passing second.

"Darren," Julian said, his voice tight, his body bristling with anger and fear. "What do you want?"

Darren's eyes flicked over to Emily, then back to Julian. "What I want, Julian, is simple," he said, his voice lowering to a dangerous whisper. "I want what's mine."

Emily's eyes widened, her hand pulling back from Julian's, confusion and alarm flashing across her face. She looked between the two men, her expression searching for some kind of explanation.

"Who is this?" she asked, her voice trembling with the weight of the situation.

Julian's heart raced as he turned to her. "Emily, I—"

But Darren interrupted, his grin widening. "I'm the one who made Julian who he is," he said, his voice smooth, calculated. "And I'm the one who will make sure he doesn't forget it."

The realization hit like a freight train. Julian could see the wheels turning in Emily's mind, the shock in her eyes as the pieces began to fall into place. Darren wasn't just a man from his past. He was a shadow, a dark force who had always been there, pulling the strings of Julian's life in ways Julian hadn't fully understood until now.

And now, as Darren's presence filled the room, Julian realized that the hidden agenda wasn't just Darren's—it was his own.

Thirteen

The Test of Faith

The air in the café felt thick, suffocating with the weight of the tension that had suddenly descended upon them. Julian stood there, his heart pounding in his chest as Darren's presence filled the space between them, like an invisible force threatening to crush everything in its path. The man who had once been part of his past, part of the life Julian had tried so hard to leave behind, was now standing before him, uninvited, unapologetic, and more dangerous than ever.

Emily sat frozen at the table, her eyes darting between Julian and Darren, trying to make sense of the situation. Her expression shifted from confusion to alarm, her hands clenched tightly around the edge of her coffee cup, as if she were holding onto something solid to keep herself grounded. Julian could feel her tension radiating across the table, and a wave of guilt crashed over him. This wasn't how it was supposed to be. She was supposed to be safe, away from the chaos of his past, but now, Darren had walked right into their lives, threatening everything they had started to rebuild.

Darren's smile was cold, calculated. He leaned in slightly, his eyes glinting with something Julian couldn't quite place—something dark, something familiar. The kind of look that made Julian want to step back, but he couldn't. He wouldn't. Not now, not after everything he had fought for.

"What do you want, Darren?" Julian asked, his voice low, steady, though every muscle in his body was tense with the need to act.

Darren's grin widened, and he slowly straightened up, his gaze sweeping over Emily, then back to Julian. "What I want, Julian," he said, his voice smooth, almost friendly, "is simple. I want what's mine."

Julian felt his blood run cold. His stomach twisted in knots as he glanced at Emily, who was still staring at Darren with wide, confused eyes, her mind racing to catch up with the situation.

"What are you talking about?" Julian asked, trying to control the rising panic in his chest.

Darren chuckled softly, his eyes glimmering with amusement. "Oh, come on, Julian. You don't really think you've gotten away, do you?" His tone was mocking, almost dismissive. "You can run all you want, but there's no outrunning the past."

Julian's jaw clenched. He could feel the weight of Darren's

words settling over him like a heavy, suffocating blanket. You can't outrun the past. It was a truth he had been trying to escape from for so long, and now, standing face to face with Darren, he realized that there was no place left to hide.

"You've been making a lot of noise, Julian," Darren continued, his voice dripping with disdain. "And that's not how this works. You've crossed me for the last time. You think you can walk away from everything, from me, and just go on with your life? No one gets away that easily."

Emily stood up slowly, her chair scraping across the floor. "I don't know who you are," she said, her voice shaking with a mix of fear and anger. "But I know this isn't what I signed up for." She stepped closer to Julian, placing a hand on his arm, her grip tight, as if trying to steady herself in the face of the unknown.

Julian reached out to her, his heart aching with the intensity of the moment. He hadn't wanted this for her, hadn't wanted her to be dragged into the mess he had made of his life.

"I'm sorry, Emily," he whispered, his voice barely audible. "I never meant for any of this to happen."

Darren's eyes flicked toward Emily with a sneer, before turning back to Julian. "You're sorry? You think sorry fixes anything? You've been hiding from your own life, Julian. Hiding from the consequences of your choices." His voice dropped, becoming quieter, more menacing. "And now, you think you can just waltz into some little café and start fresh? You think you can start over, pretend like nothing ever happened?"

Julian's fists clenched at his sides, his pulse pounding in his ears. "What do you want from me, Darren?" he asked, trying to keep his voice steady despite the storm that was brewing inside him.

Darren took a step closer, his presence dominating the space between them. "What I want is simple. I want you to come back. I want you to return to where you belong. You think you can play at being some regular guy, but you're not. You're a Westbrook. And you don't get to run away from that." He paused, letting the words hang in the air, thick with implication. "You don't get to just walk away from everything your family built, everything I built."

Julian could feel the ground shifting beneath him, the familiar pull of his past threatening to drag him back into the life he had tried so hard to escape. Westbrook. The name alone made his skin crawl, a reminder of the legacy he had rejected, the power that had been thrust upon him since birth. He had never wanted it. He had never asked for it. But it had been his, whether he liked it or not.

He took a deep breath, his thoughts racing. *This is it. This is the moment. The test of faith.*

He turned to Emily, who was watching him closely, her expression a mixture of confusion and concern. Julian knew what he had to do. He knew the choice that lay before him, the decision that would define everything from this point forward.

Emily was right. It wasn't about the past anymore. It wasn't about running away from who he was or what he had been.

It was about standing up and facing the consequences of his actions. And more than that, it was about showing Emily that he was willing to fight for their future, for something real, something that wasn't based on lies or deception.

He took a step toward Darren, his jaw set, his resolve hardening. "I'm done with you, Darren. I'm done with everything you represent. I'm done being your pawn." His voice was low but firm. "I'm not going back. Not now, not ever."

Darren's eyes flashed with anger, but he didn't move. Instead, he stood there, as if savoring the tension in the room. "You think this is over?" Darren asked, his voice turning cold. "You think you can just walk away from me, from what we've built?"

Julian felt the anger surge in his chest, but this time, it wasn't fear that fueled him. It was something else. Something stronger. He wasn't going to let Darren win. Not this time.

"No," Julian said, his voice steady, the weight of his words settling into the space between them. "This is just the beginning."

Emily looked at Julian, her expression softening as she realized what he was saying. She stepped closer to him, her hand brushing his arm. "Julian," she whispered, her voice full of uncertainty. "Are you sure? Are you sure you can handle this?"

Julian turned to her, his gaze steady, his voice quiet but full of conviction. "I have to. I can't keep hiding from my past. I can't keep running. I don't know what the future holds, but I know I have to face this. For you. For us."

Darren's smirk faded as Julian spoke, his expression hardening into something darker. "You think you can just walk away from all of this? From me?" His voice dropped, becoming a dangerous growl. "You're nothing without me, Julian. You're nothing without the Westbrook name. You don't get to throw all that away. I won't let you."

Julian stepped closer, his heart pounding in his chest. "You don't control me anymore, Darren. You never did. You just made me believe that I couldn't escape. But I've found my own way now. And I'm not afraid of you."

There was a long silence. Emily stood beside Julian, her hand resting gently on his arm, her presence grounding him, making him feel like he wasn't alone in this fight. For the first time, Julian felt the full weight of his decision. It wasn't going to be easy. It wasn't going to be clean. But it was his fight now. And he was ready.

Darren's gaze flickered between them, a flicker of something dark crossing his features. Then, with a slow, deliberate motion, he straightened up and took a step back. "You think you've won?" he said, his voice low, his tone venomous. "Fine. But don't think for a second that I won't come for you. You're making a mistake, Julian. A big one."

He turned on his heel, striding toward the door, and as he stepped into the street, he threw one final look over his shoulder. "This isn't over. You'll see."

The door closed behind him with a sharp click, and the room

was silent again.

Emily turned to Julian, her face pale, her eyes wide with the realization of what had just transpired. "You did it," she whispered, almost in disbelief.

Julian nodded, his heart still racing, his mind a whirlwind of emotions. But as he looked at her, standing there beside him, something shifted inside him. The fear, the uncertainty, the doubt—they all began to fade, replaced by a quiet certainty.

This was his redemption road. It was messy, it was uncertain, but it was the only road that mattered.

And he was ready to walk it—one step at a time.

Fourteen

The Sacrifice

The morning after Darren's visit felt like the calm before a storm. Julian sat in the dim light of his apartment, staring out the window at the gray sky. The rain had returned, light at first but growing heavier as the minutes ticked by. The streets were slick, reflecting the soft glow of streetlights, as if the world were covered in a thin layer of glass—fragile, fragile enough to break with the wrong touch.

But it wasn't the rain that weighed heavily on Julian's mind. It was the decision he had made. The moment with Darren had been the beginning of something larger, something that couldn't be undone. Julian had made his choice. He had chosen to stand firm, to face his past, and to confront the man who had held power over him for so long. But standing firm wasn't always enough. Sometimes, standing firm meant making a sacrifice.

The Sacrifice

And Julian knew that sacrifice was coming. It wasn't a question of if—it was a question of when.

The doorbell rang, pulling him from his thoughts. Julian didn't need to look at the clock to know who it was. It was Emily. She had been coming by more often, and though their relationship was still fragile, the quiet moments they shared had become a comfort, like a lifeline thrown to him in the midst of the storm.

He stood up slowly, his feet feeling like they were dragging against the floor as he moved toward the door. He wasn't ready for this conversation, but he knew it had to happen. They couldn't keep pretending that everything was fine. The weight of his choices, the way Darren had threatened him, the uncertainty of everything—he couldn't keep carrying it on his own.

He opened the door to find Emily standing there, her expression cautious but hopeful. Her eyes met his, and for a moment, it felt like the world stopped spinning. He could see the concern in her gaze, the worry she hadn't said aloud, but Julian knew it was there. She had felt the shift too, the unspoken change that had settled between them since Darren's appearance.

"Hey," Emily said softly, stepping inside without waiting for an invitation. "I wanted to check on you."

Julian nodded, his throat tightening as he stepped aside for her to enter. "I'm okay," he said, his voice hoarse, though he wasn't sure if he was trying to convince her or himself. He led her into the living room, where they both sat on the couch in silence.

The rain outside began to pour harder, the sound of it tapping against the windows like an incessant reminder of the pressure they were under.

Emily broke the silence first. "You've been distant lately, Julian. I can feel it. Something's going on, and I don't know what it is, but I know it's not good."

Julian stared down at his hands, his fingers twitching nervously. He wanted to tell her, to let her in completely, but there was something inside him that held him back. A part of him that was still afraid of the consequences. He had spent so long building walls around his life, around his feelings, that even now, as he looked at her—his anchor, the one person who had come to mean everything to him—he couldn't find the courage to speak.

"Emily, I..." He stopped himself, his words trailing off. He couldn't explain. Not yet.

Emily's eyes softened, and she reached out, her hand brushing his. It was a small gesture, but it meant everything to him. She had always been patient, always been there, even when he had kept so much from her. But this time, it was different. This time, she wasn't going to let him hide.

"Julian," she said quietly, her voice steady, "I need you to be honest with me. I can't keep guessing. What's really going on? I know something is wrong, and I can't just sit here and pretend I don't feel it. You can't keep shutting me out."

The words hit him like a punch to the gut. He had been shutting her out, hadn't he? He had been holding everything in, afraid that the truth would shatter whatever fragile connection they had left. But the truth was the only thing that could fix what had been broken. He couldn't keep lying, not to her.

Taking a deep breath, Julian finally spoke, his voice shaking slightly. "I've been trying to protect you. I thought if I kept you in the dark, if I kept the truth from you, you'd be safe. But I can't do that anymore. You deserve to know the whole truth, Emily. You deserve to know who I really am and what I've been running from."

Her eyes searched his face, but she said nothing, just waiting for him to continue. The air between them was thick with anticipation, but he couldn't delay it any longer.

"Darren," Julian said, his voice almost a whisper. "Darren's been controlling my life for years. He's the reason I ran. The reason I disappeared. I thought I could start fresh, that I could leave everything behind. But the truth is, I can't escape him. I never could."

Emily's face tightened at the mention of Darren's name. "But you… you said you were done with him. You said you were free."

Julian nodded, his jaw clenching. "I thought I was. But he's always been one step ahead of me. And now… now he's threatening you, Emily. He knows about us. He knows about everything. And I'm afraid that if I don't face him—if I don't do what he wants—it's going to cost us everything."

The words hung heavy in the air, and Julian could see the realization dawning in Emily's eyes. She wasn't just looking at him anymore. She was looking at the situation they were both in, the dangerous web that Darren had spun around their lives.

"So, what do you plan to do?" Emily asked, her voice steady but her hands trembling slightly as they gripped the edge of the couch.

"I don't know," Julian admitted, his voice thick with emotion. "I wish I had an answer for you. I wish I knew what the right thing to do was. But I don't. I don't know if I can protect you from him. I don't know if I can keep you safe. And I'm so sorry for dragging you into this. I never wanted this for you."

Emily leaned forward, her eyes softening as she looked at him. "Julian, you didn't drag me into anything. I chose to be here. I chose to be with you. And I'm not going to walk away from you now."

Julian shook his head, his chest tight with emotion. "You don't understand. Darren's not just a man from my past. He's a threat. A real one. If I don't do what he says—if I don't give him what he wants—it's not just my life on the line. It's yours, too. And I can't live with that."

Emily reached out, placing her hand on his cheek, her fingers warm against his cold skin. "Julian, you've already made the hardest choice. You've already chosen to stand up, to face the man who's controlled you for so long. That's more than most people ever do. But you don't have to do it alone. I'm here.

We're in this together, no matter what happens."

Her words hit him like a wave, sweeping over him and breaking down the walls he had built around himself. He wanted to believe her. He wanted to trust that they could fight this battle together, but deep down, he knew that the price of standing up to Darren was going to be more than either of them were prepared for.

But Emily was right. He couldn't keep running from his past. He couldn't keep sacrificing his future for the sake of hiding the truth. He had to face Darren, face the consequences of his choices, and if that meant losing everything—losing Emily—then he would accept it. But he would do it with his head held high, with no more lies between them.

"Thank you," Julian whispered, his voice hoarse. "Thank you for standing by me. I don't deserve you."

Emily smiled softly, her eyes filled with an unwavering confidence that gave Julian the strength he needed. "You do, Julian. You deserve to find peace. You deserve to live your life without fear. And I'll be here, no matter what it takes."

The rain outside began to slow, the storm easing just as a calm settled between them. But Julian knew that this was only the beginning. Darren wasn't going to give up easily. The price of facing him, of standing up to the man who had shaped so much of his life, was going to be steep.

And yet, Julian knew that if he was ever going to truly start over—if he was ever going to be the man he wanted to be for Emily—he had to make the sacrifice. He had to face the truth, no matter what the cost.

It was the only way forward. And as Emily's hand rested in his, he felt the weight of the decision settling into his bones. The road ahead was uncertain, but for the first time, Julian believed that with Emily by his side, he could face whatever came next.

No matter the sacrifice.

Fifteen

The Invisible World Revealed

The morning sun barely broke through the grey clouds, casting a muted glow over the city streets. Julian stood by the window of his apartment, his eyes fixed on the world outside, though his mind was elsewhere. His heart still pounded in his chest, echoing the frantic thoughts running through his head. Today was the day—the day he would face Darren once and for all. The day he would confront the invisible world he had hidden behind for so long, the world he had been running from. But now, there was no more running.

Emily had left a few hours ago, after they had talked late into the night. She had been steadfast in her decision to stay by his side, despite the danger, despite the uncertainty. She had made her own sacrifice, a leap of faith in him that he could never repay. But Julian knew that her faith in him was a burden, one that he wasn't sure he was strong enough to carry. It felt like the weight of the world was on his shoulders, and it was all because of Darren, the shadow from his past that had always loomed large, casting a darkness over everything Julian tried to build.

He glanced at his phone, the message Darren had sent him still lingering in his mind.

"You're out of time. I'll be waiting."

The words were simple, but they carried a weight that crushed Julian's chest. He knew Darren wasn't just playing games. He wasn't here to negotiate. Darren's world was a world of control, manipulation, and fear. And Julian had no idea how deep it went, how much of his life Darren had influenced, shaped, and pulled the strings of. For the first time, he truly understood that the price of freedom was higher than he had ever anticipated.

The phone rang, pulling him from his thoughts. It was Emily.

"Julian?" Her voice sounded faint through the line, as if she were holding back something. He could hear the concern in her tone, even though she was trying to keep it steady.

"I'm here," Julian replied, his voice strained. "What's wrong?"

"I've been thinking," she said, her words coming slowly. "We've talked about your past. We've talked about Darren and what he's capable of. But Julian… I don't think you fully understand what's at stake here. What he's capable of."

The knot in Julian's stomach tightened. He knew exactly what she meant. Darren had always been a shadow in his life, but now, that shadow was becoming a towering presence, one that Julian couldn't escape. He'd been trying to keep Emily out of it, trying to protect her from the invisible world that had haunted him for years, but it was no use. Darren had already found them.

"I know, Emily," Julian said, his voice steadying with determination. "I know what he's capable of. But I can't keep hiding from him. Not anymore."

There was a long pause on the other end, and Julian could feel the weight of her silence. She knew as well as he did that the decision they had made wasn't one that could be taken lightly. This wasn't just about them anymore. This was about everything Julian had tried to leave behind, everything he had been running from.

"I want you to promise me something," Emily said quietly, her voice almost trembling.

Julian felt his pulse quicken. "Anything."

"No matter what happens," she said, her voice strong, but filled with emotion, "I want you to promise me you won't go back to him. No matter what he says, no matter what he offers. This isn't just about you anymore. It's about us. And I need you to fight for that, Julian. Fight for us."

The weight of her words hit him like a freight train, and for a moment, Julian couldn't breathe. He had spent so long trying to protect Emily, trying to shield her from the world that had threatened to swallow him whole. But now, he understood. This was the true test of faith. This wasn't just about surviving Darren's threats. It was about surviving the invisible world that Darren represented—the world of control, of manipulation, and of lies. The world Julian had been a part of for so long.

"I promise, Emily," Julian whispered, his voice raw with emotion. "I won't go back to him. I won't let him take us."

The silence stretched between them, but this time, it felt like a promise—like a bond that was unbreakable, no matter what came next.

"I'll be waiting for you, Julian," Emily said softly. "But please, be careful. Please come back to me."

The line went dead, and Julian stood there, staring at the phone in his hand. Her words had solidified something deep within him. This wasn't just about the past anymore. It wasn't just about Darren. It was about their future—about what they could build together, even if it meant facing everything Julian had tried to forget.

He turned back to the window, the rain now falling in a steady downpour, as if the heavens themselves were mourning the decisions that had led him here. But there was no turning back. He had made his choice, and now, he would have to live with the consequences.

The doorbell rang again, breaking the silence. This time, Julian didn't hesitate. He knew who it was. He had known this moment was coming, but even now, the sight of Darren standing on the other side of the door felt like the weight of the world pressing down on him.

Julian opened the door, his heart pounding in his chest as he faced Darren, who stood there with a smile that could only be described as cruel.

"Julian," Darren said, his voice smooth, as if they were old friends. "I see you've finally decided to face me. I knew you wouldn't disappoint me."

Julian didn't answer, his jaw clenched, his fists tight at his sides. He couldn't let Darren see the fear in him. He couldn't let Darren control him anymore.

"You've made your choice, Julian," Darren continued, stepping closer, his presence filling the space. "But I'm afraid it's too late. You can't escape what you are, what you were born into. You can't escape your family, your legacy. You can't escape me."

Julian didn't flinch. "I've escaped you before. And I'll do it again."

Darren's grin faded, his eyes narrowing. "You think you can just walk away? You think you can take everything I've built and throw it away without consequences?"

Julian took a deep breath, the weight of everything he had

fought for pressing against him. "I'm not asking for your permission, Darren. I'm done with your world. I'm done with everything you represent. And I'm done being your puppet."

Darren's expression darkened, his posture stiffening with anger. "You think you're in control? You think you've won? This is just the beginning, Julian. The invisible world I created—our world—isn't something you can simply walk away from. You're making a mistake you'll regret."

Julian stepped forward, his voice low but firm. "I've already made that mistake, Darren. And I'm not going back."

Darren's face twisted with fury, his hands clenched at his sides. "You'll regret this. You'll regret turning your back on everything you were meant to be."

Without warning, Darren turned and stormed out of the apartment, his footsteps loud and heavy as he disappeared into the rain-soaked world outside. Julian stood there for a moment, his body tense, his heart racing. He knew this wasn't over. It could never be that simple. But something had shifted in him.

For the first time, Julian felt like he wasn't just running from his past—he was actively fighting to escape it. The invisible world Darren represented was still a part of him, but it no longer controlled him. And as much as he knew the battle wasn't over, he also knew that he had taken the first step toward freedom.

He reached for his phone, his fingers shaking as he dialed Emily's number. The phone rang for what felt like an eternity before she answered.

"Julian?" Her voice was quiet, hesitant, as if she were unsure of what to expect. "Are you okay?"

Julian's chest tightened, but he forced himself to speak, to let her hear the truth in his voice. "I'm okay," he said, his voice steady. "And I'm not going back. I promised you, Emily. And I'm keeping that promise."

There was a long pause on the other end, and then, Emily's voice, soft and full of relief, came through the line.

"I'm so proud of you, Julian," she whispered.

The rain outside continued to fall, but in that moment, Julian knew that he had taken the first step toward something real—something that wasn't controlled by the invisible world of his past. Whatever came next, he would face it with the truth on his side.

And for the first time in his life, Julian felt like he could finally breathe.

www.ingramcontent.com/pod-product-compliance
Lightning Source LLC
LaVergne TN
LVHW051954060526
838201LV00059B/3645